A WEEKEND WITH DEGAS

A WEEKEND WITH

Degas

by Rosabianca Skira-Venturi

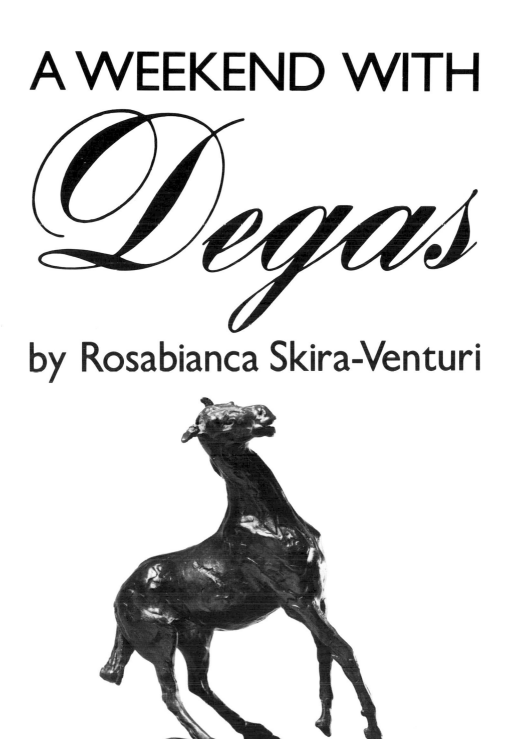

SKIRA

RIZZOLI
NEW YORK

First published in the United States of America in 1992 by
Rizzoli International Publications, Inc.
300 Park Avenue South
New York, New York, 10010

Library of Congress Cataloging-in-Publication Data

Skira-Venturi, Rosabianca.
    [Dimanche avec Degas. English]
    A weekend with Degas / by Rosabianca Skira-Venturi.
       p.   cm.
    Translation of: Un dimanche avec Degas.
    Summary: The nineteenth-century French artist talks about his life
and work as if entertaining the reader for the weekend. Includes
reproductions of the artist's work and a list of museums where works
are on display.
    ISBN 0-8478-1439-4
    1. Degas, Edgar, 1834–1917—Criticism and interpretation—Juvenile
literature.   [1. Degas, Edgar, 1834–1917.   2. Artists.]   I. Title
N6853.D33S5513 1992
709'.2—dc20   91-38364
[B]   CIP
                                                             AC

Design by Mary McBride

Printed in Great Britain

Bonjour! You caught me at a good time. Usually I'm working, but today I'm in the mood for a change and a weekend in your company suits me just fine. You're curious about my career as a painter, you say? I'm happy to tell you about it because I'd like very much for you to understand and enjoy my paintings. You see, I've always felt that paintings should have a life of their own—the more closely we look, the more they offer up for us to see. It's not easy to explain, but we have plenty of time. Just let me clean these brushes and lock up the studio. There. Now, come with me and you'll see . . .

By the way, what is your name? I am called

Edgar Degas

Look back at my self-portrait on the previous page. I was an elegant young man—the son of a banker, with a fine suit of clothes, a top hat, soft chamois gloves, a watch chain and, I must admit, an aloof expression, which I kept all my life. If someone had asked me then what I was trying to accomplish as an artist, what would my answer have been? What is my answer now? Let me share some experiences with you to help you understand.

See this painting of little Hortense? She tried very hard to hold still so that I could paint her portrait, but it wasn't easy for her! Foolishly, I had given her a sliced apple to hold—what child that age could resist such a temptation? Every time I tried to capture that little face on canvas she was chewing and her cheeks bulged with apple. I grew more and more angry and frustrated. As the work progressed, however, Hortense began to understand what a long and difficult process it is for a painter to set his colors down on canvas in just the right way.

As you can see, I finished the portrait before she finished the apple and we had a good laugh about it afterward. I wanted to capture those colors so that everybody would know exactly how that room looked and how much I loved that restless little girl, looking for all the world as impertinent and impatient as she really was! Have I accomplished what I set out to do? With every painting I've made, I've asked myself the same question.

The Portrait of Mlle. Hortense Valpinçon *shows a mischievous little girl. In the enlarged detail on the opposite page, we see close-up the embroidery spilling out of her mother's pretty sewing basket, as well as the beautifully decorated tablecloth. Degas painted this portrait between 1869 and 1871 at the Valpinçon estate, Ménil-Hubert, in Normandy, in the northwest part of France. Degas made several visits to his friends there throughout his lifetime.*

Looking as aloof and grumpy as I do in my self-portraits and photographs, you can probably guess that I'm not exactly known as a jovial fellow or *bon vivant*, as we say in France. Still, I like to enjoy myself. When I was young, I traveled all over Italy to study paintings in the museums there. The great painter and admirer of Italian Renaissance painting, Gustave Moreau, was my mentor, or teacher. He drew this sketch of me while I was visiting the famous Galleria degli Uffizi, a museum in the beautiful city of Florence. He certainly captured the serious and studious look of the good student I was. And yet, I must tell you, I also spent a good deal of time just lazing about, doing nothing! I'm all in favor of idling away the hours, just as long as it doesn't become a full-time occupation! Fortunately, a gesture, a movement, a look on someone's face, would lead me back to my brushes time and time again.

Gustave Moreau executed a number of drawings of his young friend Degas, in particular this sketch (opposite), dating from 1859, where the artist is obviously under the spell of Degas's keen mind and curiosity. The Bellelli Family (above) was painted at his aunt's apartment in Florence between 1858 and 1860. This famous work has a haunting atmosphere: each figure appears isolated from the others. For example, the little girl seated in the foreground, is she pouting? And the father at his desk with his back to us, is he angry? Even the picture frame hanging on the wall seems mysterious, as it appears to be much too large for the tiny portrait it holds.

When I was thirty-five years old, I decided to accompany my brother, René, on a trip to the United States. After a long voyage we reached the state of Louisiana, where I was fascinated by the paddleboats that traveled up and down the wide Mississippi River. The city of New Orleans was our destination, where "one does nothing . . . nothing but cotton, one lives for cotton and from cotton." My parents and brothers had business there—cotton, naturally, which didn't interest *me* a bit.

THE CHAMPIONS OF THE MISSISSIPPI.
"A Race for the Buckhorns"

The July 1863 issue of the French publication, "Journal pour tous," published the drawing opposite, depicting the backbreaking work involved in the process of cultivating and preparing cotton for the market. In the lithograph shown above, Currier & Ives, printers who worked in New York City from 1835 to 1907, illustrate a scene of the period's famous paddleboats plying the Mississippi River.

What did interest me, however, was observing them all at work in their office. For many long hours, I did studies of their attitudes and postures as they worked. Why, I even extended my stay in New Orleans, just to do that!

A number of them, as you can see, still have their hats firmly planted on their heads because they are only passing through. They don't really seem to be working together, do they? My uncle, wearing spectacles, examines a tuft of cotton, my brother, René, quietly reads the newspaper, the cashier checks the accounts and Achille, my other brother, waits in the background, leaning against the service counter. No one seems to be in a hurry. Observing and painting them in this way was more amusing to me than if I had agreed to my family's request to do each of their portraits individually!

It was an extraordinary journey for me and while I was there I wrote to a friend:

Everything attracts me here, I look at everything. I am piling up ideas it would take me ten lives to carry out. But I'll be dropping them all in six weeks, with no regrets, when I leave to return home for good. . . .

And that sums up my character; I am never satisfied.

Portraits in an Office: The Cotton Exchange, New Orleans, *is a marvelous work in which the atmosphere of Degas's family's offices is perfectly captured.*

Although I have traveled widely, it is in Paris, the capital of France, that I prefer to live. I'm a city man or, more accurately, a neighborhood man, and I become very attached to one particular neighborhood. Nearly all my studios have been in the hilly section of Paris called Montmartre and each time I have had to move it has been very sad for me.

After my trip to Louisiana, I returned to Paris and was happy to be among my friends once again and pleased to rediscover the hustle and bustle of the streets. Even when it rains in Paris, the city is still so much fun. There are always lots of things going on—some of them a bit strange—so that I'm continually tempted to leave my studio to wander the streets. I can spend hours doing this! Would you like to come with me today? We can stop at a café and have lunch. We might see performing dogs or a flea circus or a woman selling potatoes—hot and ready to eat!—and, everywhere you look, little shops with colorful windows.

If your mother were here, she might be drawn to the milliner's, where hats of all shapes and colors are to be found. I'm often drawn there too, but for a different reason—to paint. Those hats, set side by side on the counter, are like bunches of flowers, freshly picked from a luxuriant garden. Women in this shop strike such delightful poses as they study their graceful reflections in the mirror.

In At the Milliner's *(above), painted in 1882, Degas reveals his ongoing fascination with capturing an unguarded moment. At that time it was considered fashionable for women and men to wear a hat when going out. Opposite is* Paris Street; Rainy Day, *painted by Gustave Caillebotte, an artist who exhibited with Degas at several Salons. These government-sponsored exhibitions were the only opportunity for artists in Paris to show their work until 1874, when the Impressionists hung their first privately organized exhibition.*

Woman selling potatoes

Street performer with dogs

When we were young, my brother and I would dine together regularly, and we both loved going to *café-concerts*. These were outdoor cafés where popular singers of the day would perform. I found it enormously entertaining: people of all sorts crowded together, eating and

drinking, talking and laughing, scarcely paying attention to the show.

The stage, however, was alive with spirited performances. Singers had to sing at the top of their lungs to make themselves heard above the rowdy crowd. Turn the page to see my friend Thérésa holding her hands to look like paws as she sings and acts out *La Chanson du Chien*, or "The Song of the Dog." Don't ask *me* to sing it for you, though, because I've forgotten all the words.

I loved to watch the stage close up. The costumes and settings seemed so enchanting and magical beneath the bright gas footlights. In the summer, I liked to go to the *Alcazar-d'Été* or the *Café des Ambassadeurs*, elegant open-air cafés along the Champs-Elysées, a wide stylish avenue in Paris.

In the two large volumes of Paris-Guide, *published in 1867, the period's greatest writers described the major themes and critical events that marked the French capital. Naturally, they made sure to mention the balls and outdoor concerts such as the one depicted above. On the opposite page is* Café-Concert at the Ambassadeurs, *executed by Degas in pastel between 1876 and 1877. Here Degas used a device which he often employed, called "foreshortening." With this type of perspective, the painter shortens the apparent distance between the foreground and the background parts of the painting. In this painting, the rows of people are pushed together to make us feel closer to the stage, where the action of the painting takes place.*

It does not matter whether or not we know the words to the song that the woman sings in the painting opposite. It is the way she holds her head and raises her arm so dramatically that makes this portrait, Singer with a Glove *(c. 1878) one of Degas's most well-known works. In the painting above,* At the Café-Concert: "The Song of the Dog," *Thérésa delights the audience with her loud voice and broad humor. In this pastel, drawn between 1875 and 1877, Degas captures the evening's merriment and good cheer in the funny dog-like gestures of Thérésa's act.*

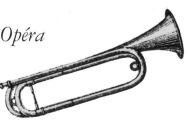

Throughout his life Degas would visit the Paris Opéra House, a magnificent building designed by architect Charles Garnier and completed in 1875. In this photograph, at the very end of the avenue, you can just see the outline of the Opéra and imagine it alive with voices and the music of the orchestra. In the portrait opposite called, appropriately enough, Attentiveness (c. 1880), *by Degas's friend Jean-Louis Forain, Degas seems to listen closely to the sounds that drew him to the Opéra.*

Here we are at the Opéra. I've wandered for hours around the grand concert hall, the corridors, and the stage wings of this Opéra House and I've seen and heard many a marvel here. One day, it was the orchestra which caught my eye. Placing myself near the pit, I found an unexpected point of view from which to paint the musicians engrossed in their playing. How fond I am of all those instruments: violins, cellos, oboes, bassoons, flutes, and trombones, a great confusion of bows and elbows and heads, bent over brass, wood, and strings!

Anyway, I could barely make out the stage where—you can see there in the background, can't you?—ballerinas danced, bright, light-filled splashes of pink and blue.

My friend the bassoon player, Désiré Dihau, once took such a liking to a picture of mine that he carried it straight home, even before I considered the painting finished. Moreover, I never like to admit that a work is completed; I'm forever changing something, right down to the last minute. I have often added a bit of color here or there. Why, I've even attached entire strips of canvas or paper to the left or right side of my painting, transforming the shape of the original surface and altering the composition. My friends and the art dealers who sell my paintings have often lost patience with me, but what can I do? As I told you, I'm never satisfied. . . .

Degas was very fond of the overhead view of musicians in the pit with the stage in the background, as seen on the opposite page, in The Orchestra at the Opéra *(c. 1870). However, it was above all the fairy-like magic of young dancers that won his heart. Here is a sketch entitled* Dancer Adjusting her Slipper *(1873).*

Degas

25

But enough of my well-known discontent, let's get back to my beautiful ballerinas! More often than not, their slight, graceful bodies were the focus of the painting, rather than a half-hidden, colorful blur in the background. In fact, they so captivated me that I can no longer count the number of drawings, paintings, studies, and sculptures I've done of them, trying to convey the grace and tension that surrounds their movements. At the school of dance, with its untidy, musty corridors and gray, high-ceilinged rooms, we seemed a far cry from the joyful, lively open-air cafés.

The dance examinations were not open to the public. However, I obtained a pass which I kept for fifteen years so that I might visit on a regular basis this austere institution with its sweaty atmosphere. In my eyes, the school was a unique place, filled with the magic of movement. It is truly an entrancing moment when a figure is poised before executing a certain step and seems frozen in place. The dance instructor's hand gestures to stay an excited, headstrong pupil; in the background, other young dancers practice a variety of movements and steps. The room is no longer a somber place—it has come alive with anticipation and the unexpected: a dancer scratches her back while another adjusts her earring, a small dog and a green watering can appear in the foreground. The room is made cheerful, too, by the glints of light that play across the dancers and their costumes as they prepare for their *jetés, balancés, pirouettes, gargouillades, entrechats, fouettés, pointes.* These words are easy for me to pronounce, but do they dance off your tongue quite as lightly? And those lovely little skirts, the airy tutus with beautiful bows in the back (those are my invention—I can't resist the urge to add my own touch) which the ballerinas wear so proudly! Such dresses make a perfect subject for a painter's brush.

The Dancing Lesson (c. 1876) is the first large-scale work that Degas painted in his career. He worked on it for quite a long time, from 1873 to 1876, often changing the painting's format and figures. (He changed the ballerina in the foreground with the green bow twice!) This picture is bathed in a pale, uneven light where each young dancer seems to be practicing for herself only.

During the many stages of his career, Degas always returned to the theme of ballerinas: at rest, at work, and on stage. Here we see three different ways he made art: pastel crayon, oil paint, and sculpture.

Opposite: Dancer with a Fan, c. *1879. Pastel. (Detail.)*
Above: The Rehearsal, c. *1874. Oil on canvas. (Detail.)*
Right: Grande Arabesque, Third Time, *1882–91. Wax.*

I think I will paint dancers all my life! I have observed them—and observe them still—from near and far, singly and in groups, their arms in the air or at their sides, radiant in performance or slumped wearily in a chair. I have constantly varied the scene and the way I frame it, depicting my dancers now from straight on, now from above, now from below, now from another unusual angle. I have varied the techniques as well.

Opposite page: End of the Arabesque *or* Dancer Taking a Bow, *1876–77. Liquid medium and pastel on canvas.*
Right: Dancers on a Stage (Danseuse verte), c. *1879. Pastel and gouache.*

Please don't think, though, that I spend all my time hard at work, far from it! As you know, I'm a true follower of what the Italians call *far niente*—that is, the secret of wasting time, doing nothing, loafing about. One of my friends, the painter Gustave Caillebotte, if not the most brilliant artist, is certainly the richest (and generous to boot!) and the most eager defender of the exhibitions that we have. (You can see a painting of his on page 17.) He has written this about me:

He spends his time at *La Nouvelle Athènes* (a famous café in Paris) or mingling with society. He would do better to work a little more on his painting. It is clear to one and all that he is right a hundred times over when he speaks. Yet . . . working, he would be much more in the right.

Well, I take his remarks to be a compliment!

The engraver Marcelin Desboutin made this etching of Degas which dates from about 1876. Musicians at the Orchestra (opposite) draws together two of Degas's favorite themes: in the foreground, musicians concentrating on their instruments and, in the background, a radiant ballerina taking her bow.

La Nouvelle Athènes was a very congenial place where everyone gathered in the years following the terrible war that devastated France in 1870. We would all meet there: painters, critics, beautiful women, and artists' models. Our Venetian friend, Zandomeneghi, has portrayed himself seated at a table with the beautiful and famous Suzanne Valadon. After having posed for many artists (including myself), she took up painting herself—with no small talent. Ah, if only those tables could talk, what tales they would tell!

By 1895 there were nearly thirty thousand cafés in Paris. This period photograph shows La Nouvelle Athènes, *located in Montmartre, Degas's favorite neighborhood. This café was also known as the "Intransigents' Café" because it was here that the Impressionists, unwilling to compromise their ideals, would rally in the days of their first exhibitions.*

The painting on the opposite page, At the Nouvelle Athènes Café (Self-Portrait with Suzanne Valadon) *was painted by Federico Zandomeneghi in 1885.*

G. C. A., Paris   794   Montmartre. —

rue Pigalle — Nouvelle Athènes.

I was born into an age of discovery, and was as relentlessly experimental in my field as scientists were in theirs. It was not long before I decided that oils were not enough for me. Moreover, I started to have problems with my eyesight, and you can well imagine that such an affliction, for a painter, is a real concern. So, partly to set my mind at ease and partly to develop my art, I tried new mediums and materials. I experimented with

all kinds of colored pencils, made engravings using new systems I myself perfected, and, for a time, I was very keen on the new "electric pencil" which, according to the inventors, was supposed to allow an artist to reproduce a great number of copies from a single drawing. Unfortunately, this technological novelty just didn't work.

Photography begging to be assigned a small space at the art exhibition.

Degas was passionately fond of new artistic techniques and materials, such as photography, although he pretended all the while to reject this exciting new medium. At the top of the opposite page you can see a Kodak box camera, made by the Eastman-Kodak Company in 1888, a type of camera Degas used with pleasure. At the bottom of the same page is a photograph of Degas and his friends in Dieppe, France, taken in 1888. Degas took this picture himself and set things up so that he could be in it as well. Do you see him there behind the lady with the closed parasol, turning his profile to the camera?

Ungrateful Painting rejects Photography's request, even though Photography has been so beneficial to Painting.

In 1858 Nadar, one of the pioneers of photography in France, took aerial photographs from his helium-filled balloon. The great painter and caricaturist, Honoré Daumier, commemorates in the print above Nadar's efforts to popularize photography. On the right-hand side of the page are three little caricatures also by Daumier, satirizing the battle that was waged to admit photography to the realm of the arts.

Two years later: Painting invites Photography to participate in the exhibition!

I also brought pastels back into fashion. I use these chalky, fragile sticks of color quite often because they allow me to recapture on paper my brightest "impressions" of the colors of life.

Ah, yes, my painting has been called "Impressionist." I can well remember all the trouble I gave myself to help organize those famous exhibitions in which my work was hung alongside that of my friends, Manet, Renoir, Monet, Pisarro, and others who were later labeled "Impressionists." But labels never meant anything to me. A famous novelist, Emile Zola, wrote:

> In short, Monsieur Degas alone has profited from the private exhibits of the Impressionists; and we must seek the reason for that in the very talent he possesses. Monsieur Degas has never been persecuted by the official Salons. He was admitted, his work hung in a fairly nice spot. However, as he is of a delicate artistic temperament, as he does not command attention with great, powerful works, the masses pass by his paintings without seeing

them. Hence, the annoyance on the painter's part, which is quite justifiable. . . .

So, I was the one who couldn't please the public! No matter.

Emile Zola was referring to the well-known art Salons. These annual exhibitions of art were an official event and to hold them in contempt was always the fashionable thing to do, although most painters secretly wanted to be included. As for me, even though I've never chased after honors, my paintings have sold. My friends and several galleries, in both Paris and America, have been regular buyers.

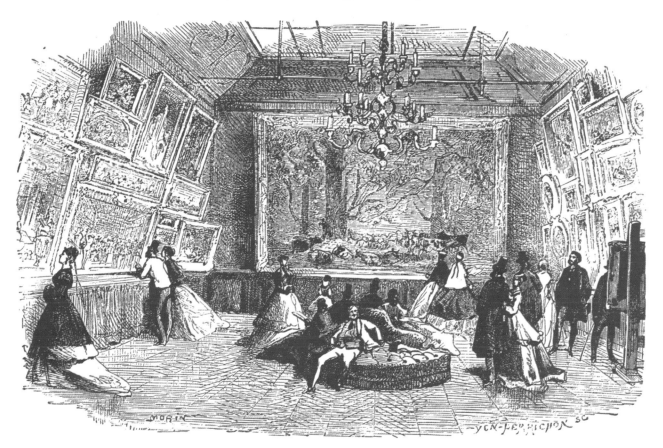

This engraving, from Paris-Guide, *shows the common practice of hanging works of art at the government-sponsored Salons so that they covered the walls from floor to ceiling. Degas and his friends were highly critical of this practice. On the opposite page, the pastel* Landscape with Cows *(c. 1888–92) is uncharacteristic of Degas's work. Unlike his friends who in later years were called "Impressionists," Degas rarely painted landscapes.*

I have a very dear friend who is an American painter, Mary Cassatt. I have portrayed her a number of times, depicting her, for example, in the famous Paris museum, the Musée du Louvre, as she studies attentively one masterpiece or another. Tall, determined, headstrong, talented, distinguished, she has been a generous friend to me; but, she is also (unfortunately) as stubborn as I am, so much so that we've had innumerable quarrels. She has encouraged a number of collectors and art dealers from her country to buy my works, and the first of my paintings to enter an American museum was my *Racehorses at Longchamp*, acquired by the Museum of Fine Arts, Boston.

These books carefully arranged on their shelves seem like so many sticks of pastel in this detail from the portrait of Edmond Duranty which Degas completed in 1879. Degas used a very special technique when he worked in pastel. After sketching his subject, he would spray boiling water over the rough drawing, transforming the colorful dust of the pastels into a paste, which he then reworked with a brush. Yet, he never worked all the areas of his composition in the same way. It is easy to understand why he was rarely satisfied with his work. In the detail at left, of Mary Cassatt at the Louvre, Degas shows further technical complexity by combining soft-ground etching, dry-point etching, and aquatint etching.

Museums were one of the few places women could go unescorted in Degas's time. In this pastel, he has used Mary Cassatt as the model for both stylish women as they view paintings in the Louvre.

In the painting on the opposite page, Woman Looking Through Field Glasses, *detail,* c. *1869–72, the woman seems to be looking at the spectacle of horse racing with the same intensity as did Degas himself. Two scenes that might very well have caught her attention are* Carriage at the Races, *1870–73 (detail, above) and* Racehorses at Longchamp, *detail, 1873–75 (right).*

Let's go together to the racetrack, you and I! I know I told you that I'm a city man but, like my friend Manet, I'm also a man who enjoys the horse races. I'm fascinated by the color and the atmosphere: the limbs of the horses and the men—their supple, limber, agile motion. I'm drawn to seek a moment of truth, when motion becomes suspended, and I can freeze it in time, forever. Come with me, I'm sure you'll enjoy yourself!

Tilbury

Petit duc

In this painting, Carriage at the Races (Jockeys amateurs près d'une voiture), c. *1877–80, the carriage you see is probably a* Petit duc, *the carriage of choice for transporting spectators at the races. If you were more interested in speed, you might have used the light two-wheeled Tilbury. Degas loved its elegant simplicity.*

44

I don't know about you, but the particular atmosphere just before the start of a race makes me nervous and excited and leaves me completely under its spell. It's an exceptional moment: a horse rears up, a rider makes for the stands, others prepare for the race or are seen leaving the field. The jockeys wear colorful silk jackets as bright as the green grass beneath our feet. The slender, dancing legs and hooves of the horses barely seem to graze the turf as they pass by. All is anticipation, everything appears poised, each rider intent on getting off to a good start.

Racehorses at the Stands, 1869–72. *Oil on canvas.*
Page 48: Rearing Horse, 1880. *Bronze.*
Page 49: The gentleman in Rider in a Red Coat, *which Degas painted in 1873, raises his top hat in salute as he quits the field.*

. . . And then? Then there are certainly thousands of interesting things taking place, but they do not become subjects for my painting!

Many years have passed since I was an impatient young man and my father said, "You have a good future before you, don't lose heart." He was right—my future proved to be a good one, but my work has never been easy! Let me say that, as an artist, I have had many rewards but also many struggles. Why struggle, you might ask? Perhaps to make us see what we fail to see at first glance. I have tried to reveal the unusual, unexpected side of things—a special way of seeing a person immersed in a task, a ballerina practicing or at rest, jockeys and horses at the racetrack, women ironing, bathing, or simply gazing at themselves in a mirror. Ordinary, everyday scenes, you say? Not for me, they're not! Anyway, that is what I've always struggled to capture on my canvases—a glimpse of a certain moment, frozen in time as in a photograph.

But you look frozen yourself, my young friend. The races are over and the sun has gone down. Let's go back to Montmartre and have ourselves a warm supper.

Throughout his long life as an artist, Degas was a tireless explorer, constantly experimenting with new media and techniques. Should you wish to explore too, and find out more about him and his work, there are many fine museums in the United States and abroad where you may do so.

WHERE TO SEE DEGAS

New York, New York
The Metropolitan Museum of Art

One of the largest and most impressive museums in the United States is The Metropolitan Museum of Art in New York City, located since 1880 on fashionable Fifth Avenue. The museum possesses a wide variety of works in different media which demonstrate Degas's ongoing fascination with the way dancers and horses move. Here you will find many paintings, sculptures, and drawings of ballerinas, including *Dancer Adjusting her Slipper* (page 25), a wonderful collection of bronze horses, as well as other important examples of his work.

The Frick Collection

A short walk south on Fifth Avenue will bring you to The Frick Collection, housed in what was once the luxurious private home of industrialist Henry Clay Frick (1849–1919). The mansion contains a magnificent collection of masterpieces, including *The Rehearsal*, painted by Degas in 1879.

Boston, Massachusetts
Museum of Fine Arts

Just a short tram ride from the center of Boston is the Museum of Fine Arts, which has a substantial collection of paintings by Degas and his contemporaries. Here you will find both *Carriage at the Races* and *Racehorses at Longchamp* (detail) which are reproduced on page 43.

Isabella Stewart Gardner Museum

Be sure to stop in across the street from the Museum of Fine Arts to see this museum, housed in an Italianate *palazzo* or palace, with two works by Degas in its collection: *Josephine Gaujelin* (1867) and *The Weighing In* (1862–66).

Fogg Art Museum

Just across the Charles River in Cambridge, you'll find this museum on the Harvard University campus, where you can see the forceful and famous *Singer with a Glove* (page 20).

During his long and creative lifetime, Degas produced a vast body of work. In addition to the works discussed and seen in this book, there are hundreds of others for you to discover in other museums and collections scattered throughout the United States. At the Minneapolis Institute of Arts in Minneapolis, Minnesota, you can admire the entire *Portrait of Mlle. Hortense Valpinçon*, shown in the details on pages 8 and 9. The National Gallery of Art, in Washington, D.C., has many of Degas's original works, as does the Art Institute of Chicago, in Illinois. In addition, the Norton Simon Art Foundation in Pasadena, California, has an extensive collection of Degas's work, including the lovely sculpture, *The Little Fourteen-Year-Old Dancer*, with its gauze tutu and satin hair ribbon.

Paris, France
Musée d'Orsay

If you are lucky enough to go to Paris one day, don't miss the exciting Musée d'Orsay. This museum, devoted to nineteenth-century art, is one of the most important in Paris and houses many works created by Degas and his friends. Originally a railroad station, the building was erected in the center of Paris between 1898 and 1900.

Degas himself may have boarded a train here to travel to the southwest of France. In the photograph on page 50, you can see the soaring ceilings of the original structure. Here you can get to know for yourself famous works such as *The Bellelli Family* (page 11), *The Orchestra at the Opéra* (page 24), *The Dancing Lesson* (page 27), *Racehorses at the Stands* (page 46–47), and many, many others.

Musée Gustave Moreau

You will remember that Degas was a young man when he met the painter Gustave Moreau (see page 10). From this meeting there remain several portraits of Degas drawn in crayon by Gustave Moreau, whose ancient studio and Parisian apartment have been converted into a museum containing many of his paintings and drawings.

Pau, France
Musée des Beaux-Arts

The famous *Portraits in an Office: The Cotton Exchange, New Orleans*, reproduced on pages 14 and 15 was exhibited in Pau, a small town in southwestern France in 1878, and acquired later that year by the town museum. The pride that Degas felt at the sale shines through in a letter written to the curator: "I must thank you heartily for the honor you have bestowed upon me. I must also admit that this is the first time a museum has accorded me this distinction. I am pleasantly surprised and pleased by this." The painting was highly criticized at the time, but also received some praise, which was unusual for Impressionist paintings of the day.

IMPORTANT DATES
IN THE LIFE OF DEGAS

1834   Birth in Paris, France, of Hilaire Germain Edgar De Gas (later he decides to spell his name Degas as one word). His father is a well-to-do banker and a cultivated man, a lover of music and painting. He will have two sisters and two brothers. His mother, daughter of a Creole family in New Orleans, dies when Degas is thirteen years old.

1854–   The young Edgar goes to Naples to stay with his uncle,
1860   Achille. During these five years he makes several journeys throughout Italy. He goes to Rome, where he copies the frescoes of Michelangelo in the Sistine Chapel. In Florence, he stays with the family of his favorite aunt, Laura Bellelli. He also visits Viterbo, Orvieto, and Venice.

1861   Degas returns to Paris. "Edgar works very hard without seeming to," writes his brother. He enrolls as a copyist at the Louvre, where he meets Edouard Manet, around whom the young painters and critics gather.

1867   The year of the great Universal Exposition at the Champ de Mars in Paris.

1870   When war breaks out Degas enlists as a volunteer in the National Guard; he is under the command of Henri Rouart, an art collector and painter, who becomes one of his best friends.

1872   His paintings begin to be appreciated. In October, he leaves with his brother for New Orleans where his family has an important cotton business. To reach his destination, he travels ten days by boat and four days by train.

1873   He returns to Paris, bringing with him the painting *Portraits in an Office: The Cotton Exchange, New Orleans*, later bought by the Musée de Pau, a sale which pleases Degas greatly.

1874   Degas plays an active part in the preparation of the first exhibition of the photographer Nadar, which is ridiculed by the public and panned by the press.

1875   His uncle Achille dies in Naples, leaving enormous debt, causing severe financial problems to the family.

1876   Second exhibition of the Impressionists: "Degas shines. Everything else is senseless, completely senseless and ugly," writes one critic. In spite of his attachment to his group of friends, Degas is considered more and more an outsider.

1880   Degas continues to paint ballet scenes, which are much appreciated by art collectors. He also executes small sculptures in wax, one of which, *The Little Fourteen-Year-Old Dancer*, exhibited in 1881, sparks a controversy. Through his good friend, the painter Mary Cassatt, he sells several paintings to American collectors. In Paris, the ardent defender of the Impressionists, Durand-Ruel, buys a Degas pastel or oil "at a good price" every month.

1885   Degas experiments with a number of new techniques, mixing pastels with liquid medium and adding drawing materials and printing ink to his repertoire. He makes a short trip to Dieppe where he meets the young Paul Gauguin, who is disagreeable to him. In spite of this Degas admires his painting; later he convinces Durand-Ruel to mount an exhibit of Gauguin's work, and even buys a few of them for himself.

1886   The preparation of the eighth exhibition of the Impressionists gives rise to serious disagreements among members of the group.

1889   Degas is working hard and his paintings are selling, but he is far from happy: "Even this heart is artifice, the ballerinas have stitched it a cover of pink satin, faded satin—like their dance slippers," he writes in a melancholy mood. He is, however, leading a worldly existence. On a trip to Spain, he sees a bullfight. And later in the year he goes to Burgundy with a friend in a Tilbury drawn by a white horse. In memory of this trip, he does several monotypes, another one of his experimental techniques.

1895   Degas is interested in photography and often experiments with it. He is enthusiastic about the painting of his contemporaries. "I buy, I buy, I simply can't stop myself," he says; and in fact, he buys the works of Van Gogh, Cézanne, Delacroix, Ingres, etc. It becomes more and more difficult for him to work as his eyesight deteriorates, but his canvases command higher and higher prices.

1917   September 27th, he dies at the age of 84, nearly blind, having led for the last few years the life of a recluse.

LIST OF ILLUSTRATIONS

In the following list, the exact titles of the works of art reproduced in this book, the materials used in executing them, and their location are given. A work's dimension are given in both inches and centimeters, first by height, then width.

Note: the abbreviation RMN: *Réunion des Musées Nationaux.*

Cover:

Carriage at the Races, detail, 1870–73. Oil on canvas, 14⅜ x 22" (36.5 x 55.9 cm.). 1931 Purchase Fund. Courtesy of Museum of Fine Arts, Boston, Massachusetts.

Page 5

Landscape sketch. Brown ink and wash with white highlights, page of a notebook, 10 x 8⅛" (25.4 x 20.5 cm.). Bibliothèque Nationale, Paris, France.

Page 6

Self-Portrait (Degas saluant), c. 1862. Oil on canvas, 35⅞ x 28⅜" (91 x 72 cm.). Foundation Calouste Gulbenkian, Lisbon, Portugal.

Pages 8–9

Portrait of Mlle. Hortense Valpinçon, c. 1869–71. Oil on canvas, 29⅝ x 43½" (76 x 110.8 cm.). The Minneapolis Institute of Arts, Minneapolis, Minnesota (Museum Photo).

Page 10

Gustave Moreau (1826–1898): *Degas at the Uffizi,* 1859. Drawing, 6 x 3⅜" (15.3 x 9.4 cm.). Musée Gustave Moreau, Paris, France.

Page 11

The Bellelli Family, c. 1858–60. Oil on canvas, 78¾ x 98⅜" (200 x 250 cm.). Musée d'Orsay, Paris, France (Photo RMN, Paris).

Page 12

The Industry of Cotton, illustration from "Journal pour tous" (French publication), 1863.

Page 13

Currier & Ives (1835–1907): *The Champions of the Mississippi,* 1866. Hand-colored lithograph, 18⅜ x 27¾" (46.7 x 70.5 cm.). New York, New York.

Pages 14-15

Portraits in an Office: The Cotton Exchange, New Orleans, 1873. Oil on canvas, 28¾ x 36¼" (73 x 92 cm.). Musée des Beaux-Arts, Pau, France (Photo Giraudon).

Page 27

The Dancing Lesson, c. 1876. Oil on canvas, 33½ x 29½" (85 x 75 cm.). Musée d'Orsay, Paris, France (Photo André Held, Ecublens).

Page 28

Dancer with a Fan, c. 1879. Pastel. Private Collection.

Page 29

The Rehearsal, c. 1874. Oil on canvas, 26 x 39⅜" (58.4 x 83.8 cm.). The Burrell Collection, Glasgow Museums and Art Galleries, Glasgow, Scotland (Museum Photo).

Page 29

Grande Arabesque, Third Time (second study), 1882–91. Wax, h. 14⅛" (36 cm.). Musée d'Orsay, Paris, France.

Page 30

End of the Arabesque or *Dancer Taking a Bow,* 1876–77. Liquid medium and pastel on canvas, 26⅜ x 15" (67 x 38 cm.). Musée d'Orsay, Paris, France.

Page 31

Dancers on a Stage (Danseuse verte), c. 1879. Pastel and gouache, 26 x 14⅛" (66 x 36 cm.). Collection Thyssen-Bornemisza, Lugano, Switzerland (Museum Photo).

Page 32

Musicians at the Orchestra, 1870–71. Oil on canvas, 27⅛ x 19¼" (69 x 49 cm.). Städelsches Kunstinstitut, Frankfurt, Germany.

Page 33

Marcelin Desboutin (1823–1902): *Portrait of Degas, c.* 1876. Etching. Bibliothèque Nationale, Paris, France.

Page 34–35

La Nouvelle Athènes café in Montmartre (rue Pigalle). Paris, France. Photograph.

Page 35

Federico Zandomeneghi (1841–1917): *At the Nouvelle Athènes Café (Self-Portrait with Suzanne Valadon),* 1885. Oil on canvas, 35⅜ x 27½" (90 x 70 cm.). Private Collection.

Page 36

Kodak box camera, manufactured by George Eastman in 1888. Musée Suisse de l'Appareil Photographique, Vevey, Switzerland (Museum Photo).

Page 36

Degas and friends at Dieppe, France, *c.* 1889. Photographed by Degas.

Page 37

Honoré Daumier (1808–1879): *Nadar Elevating Photography to the Height of Art.* Lithograph from "Le Boulevard," (French publication), May 25, 1862. Bibliothèque Nationale, Cabinet des Estampes, Paris, France.

Page 37

Honoré Daumier (1808–1879): *Photography begging to be assigned a small space at the Beaux-Arts Exhibition.* Caricatures from the "Petit journal pour rire" (French publication), 1855. Bibliothèque Nationale, Cabinet des Estampes, Paris, France.

Page 38

Landscape with Cows, c. 1888–1892. Pastel on paper, 10¼ x 14" (26 x 35.5 cm.). Private Collection.

Page 39

The Goupil Gallery, illustration from *Paris-Guide,* 1867. Drawing by E. Morin, engraving by M. Yon-Perrichon.

Page 40

Edmond Duranty, 1879. Gouache and pastel, 39⅜ x 39⅜" (100 x 100 cm.). The Burrell Collection, Glasgow Museums and Art Galleries, Glasgow, Scotland.

Page 40

Mary Cassatt at the Louvre: The Etruscan Gallery, 1879–80. Etching, aquatint, and drypoint. Second state, 10½ x 9⅝" (26.7 x 24.5 cm.). Musée d'Orsay, Paris, France.

Page 41

At the Louvre Museum (Miss Cassatt), c. 1879. Pastel, 28 x 21¼" (71 x 54 cm.). Private Collection.

Page 42

Woman Looking Through Field Glasses, c. 1869–72. Pencil and *essence,* 12¼ x 7½" (31 x 19 cm.). The Burrell Collection, Glasgow Museums and Art Galleries, Glasgow, Scotland (Museum Photo).

Page 43

Carriage at the Races, 1870–73. Oil on canvas, 14⅜ x 22" (36.5 x 55.9 cm.). 1931 Purchase Fund. Courtesy of Museum of Fine Arts, Boston, Massachusetts.

Page 43

Racehorses at Longchamp, 1873–75. Oil on canvas, 13⅜ x 16⅜" (34.1 x 41.8 cm.). Courtesy of Museum of Fine Arts, Boston, Massachusetts.

Page 44

Illustrations from the *Nouveau Petit Larousse Illustré,* © 1924 by the Librairie Larousse, Paris, France.

Pages 44–45

Carriage at the Races (Jockeys amateurs près d'une voiture), c. 1877–80. Oil on canvas, 26 x 31⅞" (66 x 81 cm.). Musée d'Orsay, Paris, France (Photo RMN, Paris).

Pages 46–47

Racehorses at the Stands, 1869–72. Oil on canvas, 18⅛ x 24" (46 x 61 cm.). Musée d'Orsay, Paris, France (Photo André Held, Ecublens).

Page 48

Rearing Horse, 1880. Bronze, h. 28⅜" (31.3 cm.). Musée d'Orsay, Paris, France.

Page 49

Rider in a Red Coat, c. 1864–1873. Brown wash heightened with white and *essence* on pink paper, 17⅛ x 10⅞" (43.6 x 27.6 cm.). Musée du Louvre, Cabinet des Dessins, Paris. France.

Also available in this series:

A Weekend with . . .
Renoir
Picasso
Rembrandt